W9-DIJ-187

Measurement

This math series is dedicated to Nick, Tony, Riley, and Hailey.

Published by The Child's World®
PO Box 326
Chanhassen, MN 55317-0326
800-599-READ
www.childsworld.com

Design and Production:
The Creative Spark, San Juan Capistrano, CA

Photos: © David M. Budd Photography.

Library of Congress Cataloging-in-Publication Data
Pistoia, Sara.
  Measurement / by Sara Pistoia.
     p. cm. — (Mighty math series) (Easy reader)
Includes index.
Summary: Simple text describes the basic units of measurement and how to
use tools to help measure objects.
  ISBN 1-56766-115-7 (lib. bdg. : alk. paper)
 1. Mensuration—Juvenile literature. [1. Measurement.] I. Title. II. Series.
 III. Easy reader (Child's World (Firm))
  QA465 .P55 2002
  530.8—dc21
                              2001008331

Measurement

Sara Pistoia

The
Child's
World

Why do we measure things?

We measure things to find out how big they are. We can measure almost anything.

Hi! I'm Math Mutt! I'll help you learn about measurement.

How tall are you?

How much does your dog weigh?

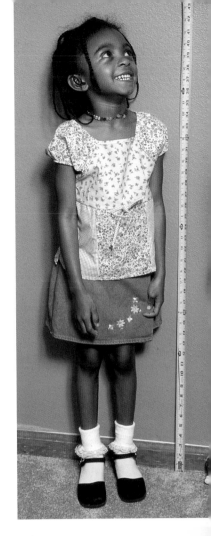

How much milk do you want?

You can measure it!

We can use simple things to measure. We can use our hands. We can use a cup. We can even use a paperclip.

Each of these things can be a unit of measure.

You need to say what unit of measure you are using.

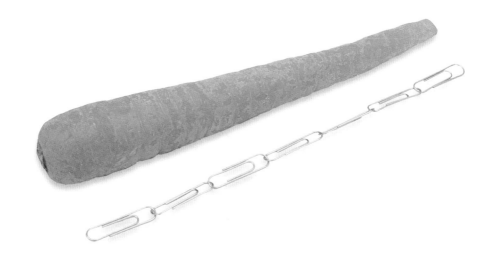

Let's measure a carrot. This carrot is about seven long. Seven long? No! This carrot is about seven *paperclips* long.

Let's measure some water. This bucket holds ten. Ten what? Ten *teacups!*

Now measure a desk with your hands. Did you measure about six or seven hands wide? Did you measure about ten hands long?

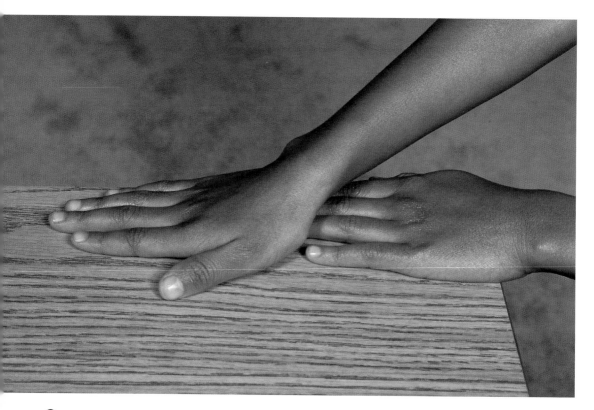

Find a grown-up to measure the desk.

A grown-up's hands are bigger than your hands. Now the desk is only four hands wide.

We need units of measure that do not change when different people use them.

We need units of measure that are the same for everyone.

We need measuring tools.

How many of these tools can you find at home or school?

Everyone can use these tools, and the measurements will stay the same!

Did you find a ruler? This ruler measures in units called inches. Let's measure the carrot again! The ruler says the carrot is eight inches long.

We use a ruler to find out how long, wide, high, or deep something is. This ruler is twelve inches long. Twelve inches is the same as one foot!
A foot is another unit of measure.

What if you want to measure something bigger than a carrot?

A yardstick is as long as three rulers. You can use a yardstick to measure something bigger.

Now measure the desk with a yardstick. Ask a grown-up to measure it, too. You agree! The desk is eighteen inches wide.

Choose the best tool to measure things. Use a ruler for small things.

Use a yardstick for big things. Would you use a ruler or a yardstick to measure a candy bar? A flag?

The right measuring tool makes our job quick and easy!

We can measure this teddy bear in inches. He is taller than the twelve-inch ruler. He is about fourteen inches tall.

But how big is the teddy bear's head? You can use a tape measure to find out. It can go around the teddy bear's head.

A tape measure can measure things that are round.

17

Do you want to know how heavy something is? You can't use a ruler. You can't use a tape measure.

Do you know how much you weigh? What tool can you use to find out?

You can use a scale! You can find a scale at a grocery store. Many foods are measured in ounces or pounds.

You can measure your dog on a scale, too! Wow! This dog weighs 105 pounds!

Wet things like milk or water are called liquids. How do you measure liquids?

Dry things like sugar and cereal are called solids. How do you measure solids?

Do you want to make chocolate chip cookies? Use these tools to measure the things you need!

There are other units of measure for food, too.

You can buy a gallon of milk.

You can buy a cup of yogurt.

You can buy a quart of ice cream.

There are so many things to measure!

How tall are you? How much do you weigh? How much ice cream can you eat?

Now let's make some cookies!

Just remember: Choose the right tool when you measure something. It makes the job as easy as one, two, three!